THE
BUBBLE WRAP®
BOOK

Also by Joey Green

Polish Your Furniture with Panty Hose

Paint Your House with Powdered Milk

Wash Your Hair with Whipped Cream

Also by Tim Nyberg

The Duct Tape Book

The WD-40 Book

How to Get Rid of a Telemarketer

THE BUBBLE WRAP® BOOK

Joey Green *(The Spam Guy)*
and Tim Nyberg *(The Duct Tape Guy)*

HarperPerennial
A Division of HarperCollins*Publishers*

THE BUBBLE WRAP® BOOK. Copyright © 1998 by Joey Green and Tim Nyberg. All rights reserved. Printed in the United States of America. No part of this book may be used or reproduced in any manner whatsoever without written permission except in the case of brief quotations embodied in critical articles or reviews. For information address HarperCollins Publishers, Inc., 10 East 53rd Street, New York, NY 10022.

HarperCollins books may be purchased for educational, business, or sales promotional use. For information please write: Special Markets Department, HarperCollins Publishers, Inc., 10 East 53rd Street, New York, NY 10022.

FIRST EDITION

Designed and Illustrated by Tim Nyberg

Library of Congress Cataloging-in-Publication Data

Green, Joey.
    The bubble wrap book / Joey Green and Tim Nyberg — 1st ed.
      p.   cm.
    ISBN 0-06-095274-1
    1. bubble wrap—Humor. I. Nyberg, Tim, 1953-   II. Title.
PN6231.B69G74   1998
688-8—dc21   97-37439

98 99 00 01 02 CW 10 9 8 7 6 5 4 3 2 1

For Bubble Wrap addicts everywhere.
May your Bubble Wrapture abound.

A Word from Sealed Air Corporation

Caution: BUBBLE WRAP® BRAND CUSHIONING MATERIAL IS INTENDED ONLY FOR PACKAGING APPLICATIONS. The uses of Bubble Wrap® brand cushioning material described in this humor book are not recommendations or suggestions for Bubble Wrap® brand materials by Sealed Air Corporation.

Bubble Wrap® is a registered trademark of Sealed Air Corporation of Saddle Brook, New Jersey, and is protected under U.S. Trademark Registration no. 1,247,076 for use in conjunction with cellular cushioning packaging material which contains entrapped bubbles of air or other gases.

Normally, we insist that our product be referred to as "Bubble Wrap® brand cushioning material," but the authors of this book are far from normal. Although we remain convinced that the phrase "Bubble Wrap® brand cushioning material" rolls off the tongue with the mellifluousness of a Shakespearean sonnet, we agreed not to object if the authors referred to Bubble Wrap® brand cushioning material informally as Bubble Wrap® in this book for the sake of comedy and literary freedom. However, this limited consent does not constitute either a waiver by Sealed Air Corporation of its trademark rights in its Bubble Wrap® registration and trademark or permission to the public generally or to any third party specifically, to make improper use of the Bubble Wrap® mark. No siree, Bob. Sealed Air Corporation intends to continue enforcing its federally registered Bubble Wrap® mark against any and all improper use and, in that regard, expressly reserves all of its rights. In other words, if anyone out there misuses our trademark, we'll ask Mike Wallace and the entire *60 Minutes* crew to come knocking at your door before you can say "Bubble Wrap® brand cushioning material is a registered trademark of Sealed Air Corporation." We now return to our regularly scheduled program.

Introduction

It was destined to happen. In December 1996, *Caryl & Marilyn*, an ABC-TV morning television talk show hosted by two vivacious housewives better known as The Mommies, did a show themed "Weird in America." Tim demonstrated a dozen uses for duct tape, including a surefire way for ladies to keep the toilet seat down. After the commercial break, Joey polished some furniture with Spam and cleaned Tim's toilet with Coca-Cola, duct tape still in place. Call it fate.

Another guest on the show, Brenda in the Red Dress from Ripley's Believe It or Not Museum, had brought a stuffed two-headed cow and other oddities. Her empty boxes sat backstage, overflowing with sheets of Bubble Wrap. We both looked at the Bubble Wrap longingly, tempted to pop it all. "Now there's something you two should do a book about," Brenda in the Red Dress joked.

The next thing we remember, the bartender at the Roosevelt Hotel was announcing "last call," and we had finished the manuscript for the world's first Bubble Wrap Manifesto on 827 cocktail napkins—which Tim had thankfully duct-taped together—just in time for Tim to catch his 6 A.M. plane back to Minnesota.

The Spam Guy and the Duct Tape Guy had met, and the Bubble Wrap Generation was born.

Incidentally, we did try to come up with some uses for both Spam and duct tape together. Tim proposed wrapping Spam in duct tape, but Joey pointed out that Spam already has an indefinite shelf life, and, in all likelihood, Spam would dissolve the adhesives in duct tape. Tim duct-taped some Spam anyway in the hopes of eventually finding out which lasts longer. The duct-taped Spam is securely stored in a Roosevelt Hotel safety deposit box, protectively wrapped in Bubble Wrap.

—Joey Green & Tim Nyberg

A Word of Warning

While Joey and Tim share a contagious enthusiasm for "the Bubble Wrap experience," they hot headedly disagree over one critical point. Whenever a use for Bubble Wrap calls for tape, Joey (being a purist) always recommends clear packaging tape. Clear packaging tape, he insists, originally made to hold cellophane together, does an equally impressive job adhering Bubble Wrap together. Plus, clear packaging tape is transparent, so you're not covering up the intrinsic beauty of Bubble Wrap. Tim, however, being a duct tape evangelist, always recommends that all taping be done with duct tape so you not only get the intrinsic beauty of Bubble Wrap, but also the incomparable majesty of duct tape working together in rapturous harmony. Of course, the choice is ultimately yours, "but either way," concede both Joey and Tim, "you're still sure to be delighted with the results."

The History of Bubble Wrap

Contrary to popular belief, Bubble Wrap was not invented by Mr. Bubble. In fact, Bubble Wrap was actually invented by accident in 1957, in Hawthorne, New Jersey.

American inventor Alfred Fielding and his partner, Swiss inventor Marc Chavannes, were trying to develop a plastic wallpaper with a paper backing. "We developed a process to do that," recalled Fielding, "but the guy who wanted it wasn't interested, so that left us with these sheets of bubbles encased in plastic. . . . It took us a while to figure out what to do with that—until we figured packaging was the way to go."

Fielding and Chavannes called their invention AirCap® material. It wasn't exactly a catchy name, but the inventors didn't have enough money to develop the product any further. Two years later, having raised $9,000 to fund six months of development work, Fielding and Chavannes built a crude six-inch-wide pilot machine that could make AirCap® material continuously.

The brains behind Bubble Wrap—
Alfred W. Fielding (left) and Marc A. Chavannes

Our two heroes incorporated their newly formed Sealed Air Corporation and went public. The first stock offering of 100,000 shares raised $85,000, enabling Sealed Air to began full-scale production of Bubble Wrap® brand cushioning materials in 1960—the same year President John F. Kennedy told Americans, "Ask not what your country can do for you; ask what you can do for your country."

But Sealed Air's bubble was about to be burst, at least temporarily. The AirCap® bubbles leaked until Marc and Al developed a machine to coat the plastic film with a Saran® barrier, preventing air loss. Later, Sealed Air developed a new technology where the barrier was built into the plastic film, giving the company a major advantage over its competition because the bubbles last longer and the packaging material can be reused.

Bubble Wrap kingpin—
T. J. Dermot Dunphy

In 1971, struggling with manufacturing problems, our tireless heroes recruited T. J. Dermot Dunphy to be president and chief executive officer of their Sealed Air empire. Dunphy, a native of Ireland and graduate of Oxford University and Harvard Business School, had turned around an unprofitable packaging company that made Popsicle wrappers, doubling sales in six years and attracting a lucrative buyout offer from Hammermill Paper.

Under Dunphy's direction, Sealed Air went from a company with sales of approximately $5 million in 1971 to a corporation which in 1996 had sales approaching $800 million. In 1971, by laminating AirCap® bubbles to kraft paper, the company developed bubble-lined Mail Lite® shipping envelopes and, in 1975, a smaller, less expensive version called Bubble-Lite™. In 1981, Sealed Air devel-

The first steam-powered production machine for making Bubble Wrap

oped PolyCap® cushioning, a non-barrier bubble cushioning material that provides inexpensive protection for products that don't require long-term protection.

Today, Sealed Air sells dozens of packaging materials, including Jiffy™ padded envelopes, polyethylene foams, and those absorbent pads you find under the steaks in the supermarket. The company's largest selling product is Instapak®, a system that pours a two component polyurethane liquid that expands up to 280 times its liquid volume as a foam cushioning.

In 1993, Alfred Fielding and Marc Chavannes, the inventors of Bubble Wrap® brand cushioning material, were inducted into the New Jersey Inventors Hall of Fame, alongside the inventor of Turfgrass (C. Reed Funk of Rutgers University) and the inventor of the edible ice cream cone (Italo Marchiony of Hoboken).

The Ice Cream Cone

Alternative Uses for Bubble Wrap

Unencumbered by those annoying and restrictive instructions, Bubble Wrap lends itself quite nicely to uses other than its original packaging application. Join the Spam Guy and the Duct Tape Guy as they apply their wacky inventiveness to this indispensible product.

Bubble Wrap Bubble Bath

Take an artificial bubble bath. Cut individual bubbles from a sheet of Bubble Wrap to float on top of the water in your bathtub. Then slip into a bubble bath that you can take over and over again.

Bubble Wrap Shower Curtain

Use duct tape (or packaging tape) to hang sheets of Bubble Wrap from your shower-curtain rod.

Bubble Wrap Burglar Alarm

Make a burglar alarm for your home. Lay Bubble Wrap on the floor inside your doors and windows. When a thief breaks in and walks across the floor, the "*pop-pop-pop-pop-pop-pop-pop*" will alert you to the intruder.

Bubblehead

Improvise a football or motorcycle
helmet. Wrap *massive* quantities of
Bubble Wrap around your head and seal
in place with clear packaging tape (or
duct tape). If Bubble Wrap can protect a
hand-painted egg shipped from
Czechoslovakia across the Atlantic, it can
protect your head when it hits asphalt.

Caution:

The specific amount of Bubble Wrap required to provide adequate protection has not yet been determined.

Bubble Wrap Beach Blanket

A roll of Bubble Wrap makes an excellent blanket at the beach.

Bubble Wrap Insect Repellent

Prevent mosquito bites on arms and legs by covering your extremities in Bubble Wrap. When mosquitoes do try to bite you, the Bubble Wrap bubble will pop and the tiny explosion of air will send the mosquito spiraling through the air.

THE
BUBBLE WRAP®
BOOK

Bubblemusic

Make won'erful, won'erful music by feeding a sheet of Bubble Wrap onto the player piano roll. Gives old-time music that up-to-the-minute "pop" sound.

Bubble Wrap Pop-A-Phone

Make a musical instrument by grabbing your xylophone sticks and hitting those bubbles. You'll be playing "pop music" like a pro!

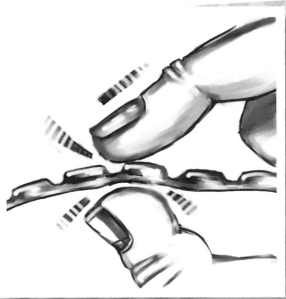

Pop Your Stress Bubble

Relieve stress. Pop a sheet of Bubble Wrap and tension magically disappears.

A Word from Our "Pop Psychologist"

"Popping the bubbles on a sheet of Bubble Wrap is actually a very effective method of relieving stress. Visualize a dab of your stress encapsulated in each individual bubble. Popping that bubble releases the stress into the atmosphere, where it quickly vaporizes—leaving you virtually stress-free. If everyone had Bubble Wrap, there'd be fewer stressed-out people scaling ten-stories buildings with semiautomatic weapons!"

—*"Dr." Bubba Rapp, Pop Psychologist*

Bubble Wrap Butt-Saver

Cushion those hard bleacher seats, at baseball or football games. Bring along a sheet of Bubble Wrap and wrap the bench for a more comfortable seat. Better yet, wear a few sheets inside the seat of your pants so you don't forget to take that valuable sheet of Bubble Wrap home after the game.

Bubble Wrap Bonus Hint for Cheeseheads

Triple-wrap your body with Bubble Wrap for warmth during those frigid games on the frozen tundra of Lambeau Field. Heated up with excitement? Start popping those insulating bubbles.

Emergency Transportation

Make a life raft. The Professor could have gotten all seven castaways off Gilligan's Island—if only they had a few rolls of Bubble Wrap to make this already inflated life raft. Ahoy, little buddy!

Never make a
deep-sea diving
suit out of
Bubble Wrap.

Sweet Dreams

Sleeping while camping can be a real
pain in the back, unless you are carrying
a lightweight six-foot roll of Bubble
Wrap as a mat to place under your
sleeping bag. Or fold a twelve-foot-long
piece of Bubble Wrap in half and duct
tape the sides to make the padded sleeping bag of your dreams.

Caution:
If you are sleeping on the beach, high tide may cause you to float out to sea.

Auto Collision Insurance

Protect your car from injury when you run into trees. Wrap your car entirely in Bubble Wrap.

The Environmentalist's View

Protect trees from car accidents. Wrap Bubble Wrap around the trunks of trees.

Bubble Wrap Krispies

Practical Jokers: Put the snap, crackle, pop back into your soggy Rice Krispies. Simply hold a sheet of Bubble Wrap under the breakfast table and pop the bubbles to convince everyone else at the table that your Rice Krispies are still going strong.

Duffer's Bubbletraps

Make "bubbletraps" when playing golf in the office. Cut out kidney shapes from Bubble Wrap and place them on the carpeting to make office golf more challenging.

Land in
a bubble
trap?
Take out
that
popping
wedge!

A Surefire Excuse!

Paint a small sheet of Bubble Wrap with red rouge and dab on your face to simulate measles or chicken pox. It's a foolproof way to get out of work or school.

Bubble Wrap Boob Job

Enlarge your breasts. Padding a bra with Bubble Wrap gives a nice natural feeling without the nasty side effects of silicone implants.

Warning: Do not substitute Bubble Wrap for silicone implants during plastic surgery.

Pop Tent

Bubble Wrap makes an excellent material for a tent. The bubbles actually provide insulation, and the clear plastic allows you to sleep under the stars, viewing the stars through bubbles.

Caution:
Not
compatible
with
porcupine-
infested
woods.

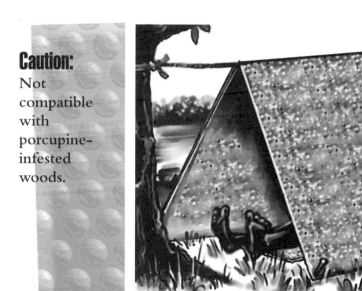

Winter Got You in Its Grip?

Insulate your house. Line the walls with Bubble Wrap "wallpaper." Not only will you be warmer, but you won't hurt yourself when you go crazy with cabin fever and start bouncing off the walls.

Among journalists, "Bubble Wrap" is slang for a news story or magazine article of little substance or consequence, a superficial piece filled with fluff or padded material.

Bubble Wrap Pharmacy

Store aspirin. Slice open each bubble with a razor blade and store individual aspirin tablets. For those chocoholics who need periodic doses of chocolate, this hint works equally well with M&M's.

Bubble Wrap Bottom Buffer

Cushion your toilet seat. Cut out safety seats from Bubble Wrap.

Fifty-year-old Farrah Fawcett appeared on the cover of the July 1997 issue of *Playboy* wrapped in Bubble Wrap, perhaps explaining how the incredibly fit Charlie's Angel stayed so well preserved after leaving the detective drama in 1977.

Bubble Wrap Softball

Turn any hardball into a softball. Wrap it in Bubble Wrap, secured with duct tape (or clear packaging tape). With a little practice, you'll be hitting "pop flies" in no time. You can also wrap your bat in Bubble Wrap for that dramatic popping sound with every hit!

Bubble Wrap Formal Attire

Tailor a Bubble Wrap tuxedo or formal dress. You'll be the talk of the town in this attractive, see-through Bubble Wrap suit or dress. Fellow partygoers will go crazy for the chance to pop your outfit.

Make Pop a Pop-able Tie

Here's the ultimate gift for the man who has everything! Make him a Bubble Wrap necktie or bow tie.

Toddler-Proof Your Glass Menagerie

Baby-proof knickknacks in Bubble Wrap to prevent breakage. Bubble Wrap also adds a touch of class to your bric-a-brac. And, in case of earthquake, your valuable Hummel collection will be handsomely protected.

Popable Place Mats

Make Bubble Wrap place mats. Guests can start popping the bubbles during lulls in the dinner conversation. You can also cut strips of Bubble Wrap and tape them into circles for matching napkin rings.

Shoe and Shine Saver

When going on a trip, roll up Bubble Wrap and put it inside and around your just-shined dress shoes to prevent them from being scuffed and squashed.

Create a Hi-Tech Decor

Decorate your home to look like a pseudo-New Wave-Sprockets-Danceteria-discotheque. Crumple up large sheets of Bubble Wrap and tape it to the walls. Be sure to run long strings of blinking Christmas lights underneath the Bubble Wrap to create a groovy glow.

Bubblecreeper

Pad your "creeper" for comfort while working under the car. As an extra precaution, tape a sheet of Bubble Wrap to your forehead. In case you suddenly lurch upward, it will prevent the undercarriage of your car from being firmly imbedded in your forehead.

Bubble Wrap contains recycled plastic and is highly efficient because it reduces the amount of material required to protect a product. Bubble Wrap can be shredded and compacted prior to landfill, reducing its original volume by up to 85 percent. We find it impossible to believe that anyone would ever want to throw away Bubble Wrap in the first place. It's far too precious.

Downhill Bubble Wrapping

Prevent ski accidents. Wrap Bubble Wrap around your long johns and make a pad to slip down your ski-pants to prevent injuries from nasty falls.

Oops! Break something?

Make that crutch more comfortable by Bubble Wrapping the padded end.

Bubble Wrap Bubblegum

Chew on a piece of Bubble Wrap.
It won't lose its flavor, it will make that
same addictive popping noise, and it
won't promote tooth decay!

Bubble Wrap Rosary

Cut strips of Bubble Wrap and pop the appropriate number of bubbles during your "Hail Marys."

Note: This tip is not currently endorsed by the Pope. But we have heard a rumor that his pointy hat is stuffed with Bubble Wrap.

The Ultimate Air Mattress

Unexpected overnight guests can enjoy the ultimate air mattress. Just unroll a length of Bubble Wrap and cover with sheets.

Caution: Once guests experience the comfort of a Bubble Wrap bed, they may never leave.

Bubble Wrap Costume Party

No need for expensive costuming when there is Bubble Wrap at hand! Wrap Bubble Wrap around your arms, legs, and body to become: Mr. Bubble, The Sta-Puft Marshmallow Man, or the ever popular "Bubble Wrap Man/Woman."

Never wrap your entire body in Bubble Wrap in lieu of using a parachute when skydiving. Bubble Wrap will not adequately cushion your fall, no matter how many layers you use.

Bubble Wrap Bowser's Abode

Insulate your dog house. Use a staple gun to adhere sheets of Bubble Wrap inside the dog house to keep your dog warmer in the winter. He'll be the envy of every dog in the neighborhood.

A layer of aluminum foil installed under the Bubble Wrap will reflect summer sun.

Bubble Wrapping to Avoid Body Work

Prevent door dings and fender benders. Bubble Wrap your car bumpers, side panels, and fenders to prevent a trip to the body shop the next time a runaway shopping cart careens into your parked car.

Bubble Wrap Boggan

One or twenty can sled down snow-covered hills on a custom "BubbleBoggan." Simply adjust the length of Bubble Wrap sheet to accommodate more sledders. As an additional safety measure, wrap all occupants in three or four layers of Bubble Wrap to avoid bruising and broken bones should you inevitably hit trees.

Bubble Wrap Picnic Bun Buffer

Cushion a picnic table bench. Lay a long sheet of Bubble Wrap along the bench for more comfortable seating. You'll be able to sit long enough to enjoy another piece of Aunt Bertha's famous cherry pie.

Volley Bubbleball

Make a volleyball net and ball. Hang a long sheet of Bubble Wrap up for use as a volleyball net, then ball up enough Bubble Wrap to make a volleyball and seal with clear packaging tape (or duct tape). Now you can give spiked balls that extra "pop!"

Soften That Stool!

Why sit on a hard kitchen stool when you can cover the top with Bubble Wrap to make an attractive and comfortable stool cushion?

Bubble Wrap Welcome Mat

Know when guests are at your front door. *Caution: It is not advisable to "hide" your extra house key under a Bubble Wrap doormat.*

Gannets—members of the same bird family that includes tropic birds, frigate birds, pelicans, cormorants, and anhingas—don't hurt themselves diving a half mile down into the sea, because they are born with what is essentially natural Bubble Wrap underneath the skin of their necks and breasts. These cellular tissues automatically fill with air when the gannet begins a dive.

Hush Bubbles

Taping pieces of Bubble Wrap to the soles of your shoes softens any sidewalk and turns any pair of shoes into poor man's Hush Puppies. Or make Bubble Wrap insoles to soothe your sore soles. Trace your feet on a sheet of Bubble Wrap, cut them out, and slip them into your shoes. They'll cushion your feet for hours.

It's like
walking
on air—
because
you *are*
walking
on air!

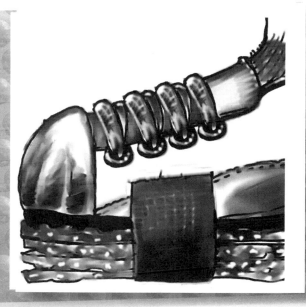

Bubble Wrap Instead of Cash

Impress your date by padding your wallet with a piece of Bubble Wrap behind your money. It will look like you have a lot more money than you actually do. Or just impress your date with the fact that you always carry around a trusty piece of Bubble Wrap.

Bubble Wrap Boat Seat

There's no need to sit on a hard wooden or aluminum boat seat again now that there's Bubble Wrap. Heck, it may even work as a floatation device if you are sitting on enough of it. Then again, it might not.

Build a Lighter-Than-Air Kite

With Bubble Wrap forming the surfaces, your kites will be more aerodynamic than ever before. Now, if you could only find helium-filled Bubble Wrap, you'd really have something!

Bubble Wrap Greenhouse

Bubble Wrap is the perfect lightweight material for building a portable greenhouse. The lightweight "skin" also provldes insulation, since each bubble works as a tiny heat-storage unit.

Quiz Time!

Can you identify this endangered plant?

Organic Bubble Wrap

Practical Jokers: Here's a plant that you can grow in your Bubble Wrap Greenhouse *(page 63)*: Cut pieces of Bubble Wrap in the shape of leaves and tape them to the branches of a houseplant. Tell guests you're the proud owner of an organic Bubble Wrap bush.

that trademark
BUBBLE WRAP
sound

There are dozens of ways to make music to the ears with a sheet of Bubble Wrap and a little ingenuity. Here are just a few:

★ Put on a pair of sporty metal-cleated golf shoes and walk over a sheet of Bubble Wrap.

★ Use Bubble Wrap to "towel dry" a porcupine.

★ Cut through a line of Bubble Wrap bubbles with a pair of hedge shears.

★ Use a pair of pliers to pop Bubble Wrap bubbles.

* Hang a sheet of Bubble Wrap from a clothesline, stake the bottom corners to the ground, and—exercising commonsense safety rules—use a bow to shoot arrows at the air bubbles.

* Tape Bubble Wrap onto the wings of paper airplanes and crash them into a camp fire for added popping and crackling satisfaction.

* Lay a sheet of Bubble Wrap on the sidewalk and use a pneumatic jackhammer to pop the bubbles. *(Warning: Unless you have exceptional hearing, it may be slightly difficult to hear the sound of the Bubble Wrap popping over the pneumatic jackhammer).*

* Fill a trash compactor with Bubble Wrap, then switch it on for an impressive symphony.

Bubble Wrap Air Bag Equipped

If your car or truck doesn't come equipped with an air bag, pack your passengers into the front and back seats with plenty of Bubble Wrap (below the neck, of course, so they can enjoy the view and still breathe).

Never use
Bubble Wrap as
a pincushion.

Live On a Flood Plain?

Cut Bubble Wrap into strips and use it to make waterproof stuffing for furniture, mattresses, stuffed animals, etc., to shorten clean up time and avoid mildew after the floodwaters subside.

Bonus Flood-Plain Hint:
You could possibly avoid flood water damage altogether by wrapping your entire house in Bubble Wrap and duct-taping (or clear package-taping) it shut.

Caution:
Actually using the Bonus Flood-Plain Hint may cause your entire house to float right off of its foundation.

Accident Prone?

Before leaving the house, wrap your entire body with Bubble Wrap to prevent broken bones.

Did you read this hint too late?
Bubble Wrap your cast to avoid further damage from banging it into walls, desktops, or friends.

Final Popping Place

If you can't afford an expensive coffin for your recently departed loved one, use Bubble Wrap to create comfortable and inexpensive coffin padding. Since Bubble Wrap doesn't deteriorate, your loving tribute will last an eternity.

The Bubble Wrap of Oz

Protect your windows and glass doors from hurricanes and tornados. Bubble Wrap each portal and secure in place with duct or clear packing tape. Come what may—flying trash cans, falling trees, airborne cattle—and your glass breakage will be kept to a minimum.

Give Me a "B"! Give Me a "U"!

To make pom-poms, simply cut two dozen strips of Bubble Wrap sixteen inches in length. Fold a dozen strips in half and tape securely with clear packaging tape (or duct tape) in the center. Repeat with the second dozen, and you're ready to cheerlead.

Venda-Bubble-Trouble

Vending machine eat your dollar bill? Get your revenge by cutting a piece of Bubble Wrap the size of a dollar bill and feeding it into the machine. There. That will teach it a lesson it will never forget!

BUBBLE
fact

According to the *Economist* newspaper, a long street in the Nipponbashi area of Osaka, Japan, lined with discount electronics stores by day, is lined with homeless people by night "sleeping on cardboard on scraps of Bubble Wrap."

Hypo-Allergenic Headrest

Cut rectangular sheets of Bubble Wrap
and stuff into an empty pillowcase.
Or, skip the pillowcase and be a Bubble
Wrap purist. Enjoy the tender caress of
thousands of tiny pleasure
bubbles against your slumbering head.

Allergic to down-filled pillows and/or dust mites? Never fear!

Banana Life Jacket

Prevent fresh fruit from getting smashed in kids' lunch bags. By Bubble Wrapping that banana, peach, or plum, you not only prevent the fruit from being bruised in that lunch bag, but you also provide your child with a low-budget kiddy meal prize—a piece of Bubble Wrap that'll make all the other kids green with envy.

You can burst "virtual bubbles" on your computer screen at the authors' Web site:

http://www.octane.com/bubblewrap.html

Bubble Wrap Garment Bag

Make a padded garment bag in minutes.
Fold a ten-foot length of Bubble Wrap
in half (bubbles in), tape the sides
together with clear packaging or duct
tape, and cut a hole through the middle
of the folded side. Slip your clothes into
the bag, slide the top of the hangers
through the hole, and—*voila!*—you've got
a nifty insulated garment bag.

Bubble Wrap Baby-Proofer

There's no need to baby-proof your house when you can Bubble Wrap the baby instead. Just remember to not cover Binkie's face, and leave an access panel in the rear for diaper changes.

Bubble Wrap Your Holiday Ornaments

Bubble Wrap breakable holiday ornaments for safe storage. Or better yet, Bubble Wrap the entire decorated tree and store it in the garage until next year.

Bubble Wrap Holiday Wrap

Wrap your Christmas gifts in Bubble Wrap. The gifts look like they are held within a million miniature snow globes. It provides hours of cracklin' good fun for the kiddies.

Bubble Wrap Baked-Good Buffer

Ship home-baked cookies anywhere in the world. Before filling a box or tin with cookies, line the bottom with Bubble Wrap. Place one layer of cookies, topped by another piece of Bubble Wrap, topped by another layer of cookies, and so on until you reach the top.

Movers' Little Helper

Pack mirror and framed pictures by wrapping Bubble Wrap two or three times around and secure in place with clear packaging or duct tape.

Bonus Moving Hint:
Line the bed of your pickup with Bubble Wrap to avoid scratching your new paint job during the move.

Never bury a loved one at sea in a Bubble Wrap body bag.

Basketball Bubble Wrap

Pad a basketball pole. Wrap Bubble Wrap five or six times around the first six feet (seven feet in the NBA) of the steel pole holding up your basketball hoop and secure in place with duct or clear packaging tape to protect players who accidentally smash into the pole.

Travelwrap

Travel light. Pack a roll or two of Bubble
Wrap in your suitcase or backpack
so you can easily carry any breakable
souvenirs you buy or accumulate along
the way. Better yet, make your entire
suitcase out of Bubble Wrap, preventing
baggage handlers and conveyor belts
from inflicting any damage.

Protective Sportswear

Sports enthusiasts can protect their
various body parts while inline or roller
skating or playing contact sports. Simply
wrap your vulnerable parts with Bubble
Wrap and hold it in place with clear
packaging tape or duct tape.

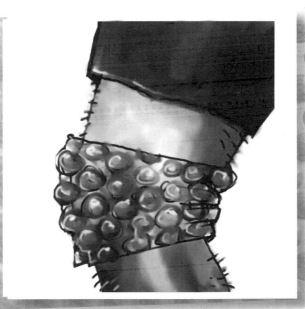

Bubble Wrap Kneelers

THE BUBBLE WRAP BOOK

Make knee pads for comfort while you wash your floors, shingle your roof, or crawl in crawl spaces and attics.

Bubble Wrap a Picnic

No picnic basket? Never fear! Fold a five-foot length of Bubble Wrap in half and tape the edges to make a strong, but lightweight picnic sack. When you unpack your food, you can untape the bag and use it as a picnic table covering.

Ant Obstacle Course

Cover your picnic table with Bubble Wrap so ants take longer to reach your food.

FOOD

Phew!

OBSTACLE

Bubble Wrap Your Bubbly

Champagne gone flat? Cut a circular piece of Bubble Wrap to float inside your champagne glass, returning the bubbles to your bubbly.

Last Call

Place the lid from a mayonnaise jar on top of a sheet of Bubble Wrap, trace around it with a grease pencil, and cut out the circles to make elegant cushioned coasters that will make all your friends jealous.

Bubble Beer Cooler

Tape Bubble Wrap around your beer or soda can. Keeps it frosty cool and looks cool, too!

Bubble Wrap Your Books

Fold Bubble Wrap over textbooks and tape (clear or duct) to make book covers that you can also pop for amusement during study hall or lulls in homeroom. A strip of Bubble Wrap also makes a fun bookmark.

BUBBLE fact

Saddle Brook, New Jersey, the home of Sealed Air Corporation, should not be confused with Upper Saddle River, New Jersey, the home of former president Richard Nixon (who, by the way, was *not* laid to rest in Bubble Wrap).

Phone Life Jacket

Protect your phone from those inevitable tangled-cord tumbles.

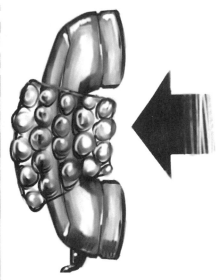

Tape a protective Bubble Wrap "jacket" around your telephone receiver.

Baby You Can Drive My Bubble Wrap

A four-foot-long sheet of Bubble Wrap placed on the driver's seat of your Pinto is a lot more comfortable that those wooden-beaded seats that never quite give you the shiatsu massage you thought they would.

Bubble Wrap Motel

Is your motel room facing a noisy highway? Can't sleep with the sound of eighteen-wheelers roaring past your door? Soundproof your room by taping sheets of Bubble Wrap over the windows.

Extra guests? Fill the bathtub with Bubble Wrap and have them sleep in it.

Bowling for Bubble Wrap

Wrap your bowling ball and all the
bowling pins in Bubble Wrap and secure
with tape (clear or duct) to make bowling
a quieter sport. The Bubble Wrap acts as
a silencer so you can better concentrate
on your game.

Bubble Wrap the Boob Tube

Tape a piece of Bubble Wrap over your television screen to make MTV hipper than hip.

Protect the Innocent

Tape a piece of Bubble Wrap over your television screen to obscure the identity of anyone on television.

Is that
Prince
Charles or
the Artist
Formerly
Known as
Prince?

The Practical Plastic Polka-Dotter

Paint polka dots with ease. Use a paint roller to paint all the bubbles on a sheet of Bubble Wrap, then use the sheet as a stamp pad on your art canvas, the walls of your nursery, dining room, or retro-sixties theme room.

············· Never
microwave
Bubble Wrap.

*(Yes, the bubbles will explode,
but so will your microwave.)*

Furniture in a Bubble

Instead of covering the living room furniture with unsightly hard plastic covers, use Bubble Wrap instead. Bubble Wrap is soft and comfy, and it actually makes your furniture look like it just came out of the box. And be sure to fold a few sheets of Bubble Wrap to make attractive throw pillows for your sofa.

The Bubble Head Look

Make a turban with a sheet of Bubble Wrap by simply wrapping it around your head and securing with tape.

Bubble Wrap Your Pickle Packs

Pack jars or bottles safely and efficiently by rolling the jar in Bubble Wrap, then sealing with the tape of your choice.

Psychedelic Eyewear

Cut circles from Bubble Wrap and tape them to your eyeglasses to create the illusion of a trip arranged by Timothy Leary's travel agent.

It's also great for simulating insect vision!

THE BUBBLE WRAP BOOK

A Cheesy Practical Joke

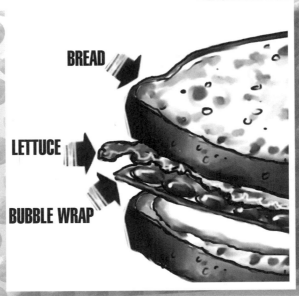

BREAD

LETTUCE

BUBBLE WRAP

Cut a piece of Bubble Wrap the size of a processed cheese slice. It adds pop to any sandwich!

BUBBLE
fact

Listen to the song "Steam" on Peter Gabriel's album *Us*, and the word Bubble Wrap will pop into your consciousness—without having to play the record backwards.

BUBBLE WRAP® substitutes

PRACTICAL:

If you don't want to waste precious Bubble Wrap for packing, use these other inexpensive, environmentally-friendly packing materials:

* **Paper Shreddings.** Use an electric paper shredder to make your own packing material, just like Oliver North did to get all those arms to the Contras.

* **Popcorn.** Simply pop corn in an air popper. Just be sure to leave out the butter and salt.

* **Quadra-Pak.** Ecopak Industries of Kent, Washington, makes short, crimped strips of paper from rejected rolls of unbleached paper used to make grocery bags.

IMPRACTICAL:

If you suddenly find yourself in the middle of an international Bubble Wrap shortage and you're desperate to use a Bubble Wrap-like packing material, consider one of these expensive, highly impractical alternatives:

* **Ping-Pong Balls and Con-Tact Paper.** Sandwich 200 ping-pong balls between two sheets of Con-Tact paper.

* **Bazooka Bubble Gum and Saran Wrap.** Blow a bubble in 300 individual pieces of Bazooka bubble gum and stick each bubble gum bubble to a sheet of Saran Wrap.

* **Soap Bubbles.** Place the breakable object you wish to ship in the middle of a cardboard box, then fill the box with soap bubbles and seal shut with duct tape.

Bubble Wrap Baby Matting

Improvise a baby changing mat. A sheet of
Bubble Wrap easily rolls up to fit in a baby
bag, and it's padded, too.

Bubble Wrap Picture Matting

Matting your fine art with Bubble Wrap makes
a statement the art world will find difficult to
ignore.

Pool-Time Fun

Make pool and bath toys. With some Bubble Wrap and tape (clear or duct), you can make all sorts of battleships, ducks, and aquatic toys that will turn bath time into fun time.

Bubble Wrap Curtain Call

Why settle for bourgeois drapes in the living room when Bubble Wrap makes stylish curtains that will make *Architectural Digest* sit up and take notice?

Feelin' Groovy?

Cut strips of Bubble Wrap and tape the ends over the doorjamb to create an awesome nineties' version of the sixties' beaded curtain that'll be totally outta sight.

Flip Out or Flip In

Flip Out: Use several layers of Bubble Wrap to make tumbling mats that have the added benefit of popping sound effects with every somersault.

Flip In: Instead of using Bubble Wrap as a tumbling mat, simply wrap yourself in a couple of layers of Bubble Wrap.

HOW TO GET FREE BUBBLE WRAP®!

Five fool proof ways to satisfy your Bubble Wrap addiction:

* Shop by catalog. You'll be inundated with Bubble Wrap. Make sure to request Bubble Wrap so you're not inundated with styrofoam peanuts (another book in itself).
* Don't overlook the most important part of your birthday and Christmas presents. The Bubble Wrap inside is often more valuable than the present it protects.
* Dig around in the dumpster behind a gift shop.
* Call packaging companies and ask them to send you free samples of their various types of packaging material.
* Write a book about Bubble Wrap, then sit back and wait for the Bubble Wrap® brand cushioning material manufacturer to send you rolls of the stuff.

Bubble Wrap-Up

Check out our Bubble Wrap Web site and send us your uses for Bubble Wrap at:
http://www.octane.com/bubblewrap.html

For information about Bubble Wrap® brand cushioning material, contact:
Sealed Air Corporation
Park 80 East, Saddle Brook, NJ 07663
Or telephone (201)791-7600

Bubble Wrap® brand cushioning material is an excellent protective packaging material. For your packaging needs, you can purchase Bubble Wrap® brand cushioning materials at U.S. post offices, mass merchants, office supply stores, and at drug stores.

Additional information about Sealed Air Corporation can be found by visiting its Web site at www.sealedaircorp.com

Acknowledgments

Special thanks to:
Our editor, Trena Keating
Jeremy Solomon, First Books
Sealed Air Corporation
Debbie, Ashley, and Julia Green
Julie, Jake, and Jana Nyberg
And to God, who invented air (without which we could not have Bubble Wrap)